WELCOME HOME

Release Addictions and Return to Love

— 25th Anniversary Edition —

WELCOME HOME

Release Addictions and Return to Love

— 25th Anniversary Edition —

Dr. Suzanne Gelb, PhD, JD

FIRST EDITION

———————

All rights reserved. This book or any portion thereof may not be reproduced or used in any manner whatsoever without the express written permission of the publisher except for the use of brief quotations in a book review.

Copyright © 2019 Suzanne J. Gelb, Ph.D., J.D.

Manufactured in the United States of America.

ISBN-13: 978-1-950764-00-6
ISBN-10: 1-950764-00-1

www.DrSuzanneGelb.com

OTHER BOOKS BY THE AUTHOR

It Starts With You – How to Raise Happy, Successful Children by Becoming the Best Role-Model You Can Possibly Be. A Guidebook For Parents.

How to Get Your Kids to Cooperate and Help Them Become the Best Grown-Ups They Can Be. (A Life Guide.)

Helping Your Teen Make Healthy Choices About Dating and Sex. (A Life Guide.)

How to Get Ready to Be a Parent and Be the Best Mom or Dad You Can Possibly Be. (A Life Guide.)

How to Forgive the One Who Hurt You Most. (A Life Guide.)

How to Deal With People Who Drive You Absolutely Nuts. (A Life Guide.)

Aging With Grace, Strength and Self-Love. (A Life Guide.)

How to Navigate Being Single and Savor Your Dating Adventure. (A Life Guide.)

The Love Tune-Up: How to Amp Up the Love That's Naturally Inside You to Enjoy Happy, Healthy Relationships.

How to Rekindle That Spark and Create the Relationship and Sex Life That You Want. (A Life Guide.)

How to Find Work That You Love When You're Stuck in a Job That You Hate. (A Life Guide.)

How to Reach Your Ideal Weight Through Kindness, Not Craziness. (A Life Guide.)

How to Care for Yourself When You're a Caregiver for Somebody Else. (A Life Guide.)

Real Men Don't Vacuum. And Other Misguided Myths That Cause Conflict in Relationships.

DEDICATION

———

If you yearn for "inner peace" — if you yearn to feel "at home" in your body, in your environment, and in your life — this book is dedicated to you.

May the pages of this book help you to find your way home — back to the infinite source of peace, creativity, confidence, and unconditional love that you were born with, that you still possess, even now, and that is waiting inside of you, waiting to be rediscovered…

You matter, too.

ACKNOWLEDGEMENTS

They say it takes a village to raise a child.

It definitely takes a village to give birth to a book, too!

So many people have touched my life, in one way or another, helping to bring this book into the world.

I'd like to thank...

- My parents, siblings, relatives, friends, teachers, mentors, ex-boyfriends, and clients — all of the innumerable people who have shaped my life through the years. Thank you for the blissful times, the peaceful times, and even the challenging times. Even the difficult, awkward, uncomfortable moments of "shaping" were valuable and taught me so much. Every experience carries with it a lesson — an opportunity to grow. For each lesson, I am grateful. Thank you.

- My support team here in Hawaii: You're so humble that you prefer not to be named, and all of the cats, chickens, roosters, geckos, occasional peacocks and rabbits, and other beautiful creatures who frolic around my property and keep me company.

- Mother Nature, the sun, air, and ocean. When I need replenishment, you are always there, infinitely giving, unconditionally loving, and you never require anything in return.

- My mentor and dearest friend, JW, for years of guidance and support (JW, I still feel your beautiful presence, even though you are no longer living here on this earth).

- Alexandra Franzen for helping me to do my best writing and for her creative insights and ageless wisdom.

- Woz Flint for her eagle-eyed proofreading.

Thank you, all of you, deeply and fully.

This book wouldn't be here without your presence in my life, through the years and today.

Thank you.

CONTENTS

Foreword by Maria N (a grateful reader)   xv

Disclaimer   xix

Introduction   1

CHAPTER ONE: Feeling the Pain   9

Emotional pain and addictions go hand in hand. This chapter offers support to heal this pain (perfectionism, fear of rejection and abandonment, self-neglect, insecurity, guilt, low self-esteem, compulsiveness, approval-seeking).

CHAPTER TWO: Learning to Heal   43

Each moment in life offers us an opportunity to change and grow. This chapter is about helping yourself step out of the addictive cycle by: taking action and freeing yourself from negative fear, erasing guilt, self-care, weeding out unhealthy relationships, playing and relaxing more, embracing positive anger, taking charge of your life.

CHAPTER THREE: Living with Love   71

This chapter is like the first day of spring — bursting with new life and fresh beginnings. Here, we celebrate being connected to our true essence — love. We embrace self-love, being free of compulsions, being fully present, self-forgiving, and supporting ourselves through our healing process. We recognize that we are not slaves to our addictions. We hold ourselves accountable for our actions, and are open to facing our feelings. We let go of fear and embrace love.

WELCOME HOME	99
Parting Words	101
Resources… To Continue The Healing Journey	103
About the Author	109
Index	113

FOREWORD

The right words, expressed in the right way, can make all the difference.

When I first heard that Dr. Gelb was revising her addictions book and issuing a 25th anniversary edition (from a friend who is a long-standing, life coaching client of hers), I thought, "No way! She couldn't possibly improve on her first book!"

Because of that book I don't overeat anymore. I don't need sleeping pills to knock me out every night. And I don't cling to relationships that are bad for me. It's been 15 years since I read that little book. It changed my life. It spoke to me.

Finally! I could stop spending money on addictions workshops that didn't work for me, self-help books that made my neurons spin with, "Whaaat! I don't understand any of this mumbo jumbo!" and so many different therapies, classes, and even 12 Step meetings… all of which — honestly — left me feeling worse than ever. "If none of this can help me, who can? What can?"

But that little book came along and changed everything. It spoke my truth to me. That changed everything. I listened to that truth. That changed everything. I'm still listening.

Up until not too long ago, I had never met Dr. Gelb (although I often catch her on the television news, here in Hawaii). So I asked my friend if she could secure an advance copy of Dr. Gelb's revised book on addictions for me. I was curious. "Could there be something more for me in this revised book?"

That prompted a little self-check. "I feel so good. So content. Am I being greedy… thinking there could be even more… thinking life could be even better?"

That's how I got to read this updated version of *Welcome Home* before it was released to the world. Wow! To me, this version oozes with even more wisdom, love, and solutions to the hell that addicts — and recovered-addicts, like me — know too well. Or perhaps the book has only been slightly tweaked, but I'm able to absorb the wisdom and love even more than I could 15 years ago — because of the value that I got out of the first book, and maybe I feel more deserving of soaking in the answers to life's challenges in this revised version.

Anyway, since I no longer over-think or obsess about what things mean, let's just say, *Welcome Home* is like a pair of big, loving arms, ready to give every addict a big hug, saying: "I understand, I'm here to help." If you feel even the slightest interest in reading it, go for it. Don't miss this opportunity.

Talking about opportunity, I'm still pinching myself that I got the opportunity to share this foreword with you.

Backstory: After I read the latest *Welcome Home*, I asked my friend if she could tell Dr. Gelb how the first book changed my life, that I loved the updated version, and that if it would help, I could write a testimonial.

What happened next was special.

Dr. Gelb called me and asked if I could stop by her office. She had something to ask me. I did. Her question? Whether I'd like to write the foreword to this book.

"Uh, me?" I spluttered. "Butttt, don't you need an addictions expert or some impressive mental health professional to write the foreword?"

She replied, "I could certainly go that route. But I couldn't think of anyone more suited to touch a potential reader who is gripped by an addiction, than someone like you, who has been to hell and back with this destructive behavior, and who found my books useful to step out of misery and into a life you love."

I couldn't hide my (happy) tears. "Uh, yes, I'd be honored," I spluttered again.

Dr. Gelb continued, with the kindest, humblest expression on her face: "I wrote this book for people who are craving answers. I didn't intend this book to be an academic text for professionals. You found answers in my books. A foreword from you would be perfect for the readers."

So that's how I got to write this foreword. Confession — reading this book can cause you to become addicted to yourself. But in the best, most loving way.

Maria N (a grateful reader)

DISCLAIMER

This book is a resource to support you in gaining a greater understanding of healing from addictive behaviors.

This book contains educational exercises and tips drawn from my career in the field of emotional wellness with over 30 years of experience. This book is for informational purposes only, and is not intended to diagnose or treat any illness, nor is it a substitute for professional or psychological advice, diagnosis, or treatment. Always consult a qualified health care professional before using any new, self-help resource (such as this one) and with questions you may have about your health and wellbeing.

Any case material that may be indirectly alluded to in this book, in articles, or in interviews [see Resources section] does not constitute guarantees of similar outcomes for the reader. No results can be promised, since everyone's personal development path is unique.

Links inside this book to external websites are for informational purposes only. Linking does not imply endorsement of or affiliation with that site, its content, or any product or service it may offer.

All link URLs in this book are current at the time of printing. Link URLs may fail at some point if the page has been deleted or moved. The author assumes no responsibility or liability for broken links.

This concludes the disclaimer portion of this book.

Let's get into the good stuff!

INTRODUCTION

The core of this book is that everything that we need in order to be happy and to handle life's challenges, is within us. That is where our strength lives.

Once we wrap our minds around this idea of self-reliance, we can release addiction — which thrives on outer-reliance (dependency on something outside of ourselves to help us cope).

Why do we "need" help with coping? How does dependency develop?

In general, we feel a void inside. (For various reasons, this is typically rooted in childhood.) This void is a lonely place deep inside... an empty chasm that aches for love, reassurance and confidence.

Because of this void, we're afraid to love, take a chance, speak up, finish a project or do something new...

It's a space that is hungry to feel safe, content, and at peace.

And up until now, we've reached for something outside of ourselves to fill up our alone, helpless, and hopeless existence.
Fortunately, no matter what your "drug of choice" (be it compulsive _____ [eating, drinking, studying, shopping, working, gambling, sex, narcotics, etc.]), generally speaking, it is

possible to reverse the compulsiveness.

I was not born addicted to ice cream (although there have been times when I've thought that I must have been!). Behavior is a choice. It is learned. **Behavior that is not serving us can be unlearned and relearned — so that it becomes an asset, not a deterrent.**

This doesn't mean that reprogramming our neurons to function more positively is easy. But it's not impossible. **And it's so worth it!**

Some people believe that, "Once an addict, always an addict." I don't.

With persistence, patience, and the right healing approach, inner peace can be achieved.

That's not to say that healing is a "one-size fits all" approach. Every person is unique.

So approaches to healing will vary — sometimes our physical chemistry may need to be balanced before anything else can be tended to. At other times, our emotions need to be healed right away. And there are many instances where body, mind and emotions can be healed simultaneously.

No matter where you begin your healing journey, there is one basic premise that applies. And it is the premise of this book, as well.

The premise?

Addictive behavior is a symptom... an indication of a deeper, underlying problem. To resolve the behavior, we need to understand what **caused** it.

Yes, the behavior (symptom) can be eliminated (hypnotherapy administered by a competent practitioner does wonders). But erasing the symptom without healing its cause offers — at most — **temporary relief** from the problem.

What happens once you identify the cause?

The inner void that propels many people to seek refuge, comfort, solace, and/or strength in a "drug of choice" (food, alcohol, sex, etc.) typically has its roots in our upbringing. We experienced something in our earlier years that gave rise to this inner emptiness. Once we identify this "something" (i.e., what part of us needs soothing, comforting and/or strengthening, and why) we can begin to heal that ache by replacing emptiness with love.

Sounds so simple. But is it really?

Yes, it is simple. But the path that got us to this point is often complex.

That's why patience is the key ... as we unravel the story of our past, so that we can upgrade our self-talk from negative to self-loving.

But patience alone won't get us to the finish line.

Desire is important. For a healing program to be effective, we must have a deep hunger to recover... **a passionate yearning to succeed**.

Searching for love.

The path to resolving addictions in this book focuses on accessing our inner strength… our true nature — which is love. This is the fabric of our being. **This is the material from which our inner home (where love lives) is built.**

Once we connect with this loving, welcoming part of ourselves, our path to recovery can flow with greater ease.

Welcome Home is intended to be a companion in the recovery process. It is not intended to cover all aspects of healing from addictions, nor can it replace the skilled input of a qualified healthcare provider, addiction support group and/or similar programs. **Instead, this book is meant to be like a good friend, encouraging you, rooting for you… and being a voice of hope for you — when that's what you need.**

I envision this book on your nightstand, in your backpack, or amongst the pile of books that can be found in your bathroom, for your reading enjoyment….

You can read it all at once… but if you do, I invite you to come back to it, a page at a time, when you feel drawn to read it. Countless people have told me that, to their amazement, there have been times when they randomly opened this book … and the page they saw was exactly what they needed to read! Magic!

Just so you know . . .

I chose to present this book in a diary format because of its personal nature — and because the hellish battle with addictions is so deeply personal. But *Welcome Home* is not a replica of any actual personal diary. Instead, the "I" in each diary entry can touch anyone who feels challenged by life and who wants stronger coping skills.

Each diary entry covers a different topic. An underlying thread unifies all the entries — **that the addiction problem is a symptom — an indication of a deeper, inner need.** A need for true inner strength.

This book addresses overcoming addictions in general. Reference to specific addictions is minimal. This is intentional — I wanted this book to be simple and easily digestible. When I was deep into my addiction, combing the shelves of bookstore after bookstore for help, the last thing I wanted was a dense, complex, theoretical book. I wanted a book that was welcoming, not overwhelming... and that's what people whom I've coached and counseled over the years have wanted, too.

I also wanted this book to touch anyone who wants to heal compulsive behavior.

And it can. No matter what a particular "drug of choice" might be (compulsive overeating, under-eating, work, shopping, gambling, studying, sex, etc.) the feelings that underlie the behavior are similar — fear, low self-esteem, sense of isolation, fear of abandonment, inability to feel or express emotions, guilt, despair, emptiness, incompleteness, sadness, difficulty standing up for oneself, perfectionism, feeling inferior at times and superior at other times, self-judgment, approval-seeking, etc.

Welcome Home moves progressively from the problem (Feeling the Pain: Chapter One) to the solution (Learning to Heal: Chapter Two, and Living with Love: Chapter Three). Simple visualizations and affirmations show us how to recognize and soothe our emotional hungers, instead of numbing our feelings with addictive behaviors. When our emotions are tended to, we can step into all that we are — magnificent, unique miracles... each and every one of us.

We have the potential for deep satisfaction, abundant vitality, and a limitless ability to love. This can be achieved when we're in touch with our true selves and we feel at home with who we really are. This book is an introduction to accessing those qualities of the glorious home within. This is the *Welcome Home* experience.

CHAPTER ONE

Feeling the Pain

DECEMBER 13

*The Perfect Person
Fear of Rejection
Survival Issues*

[Morning writing]

I close my eyes and see a circle. Inside the circle, I see an image of myself as a little girl. She looks sad and lost. She's afraid that adults don't love her. So she tries to gain their approval by being perfect…

As an adult, I still feel some of these fears. ("Will they like me and approve of me?… Will I be successful?") I still try to be perfect….

To me, the world often feels hostile, intimidating and unwelcoming. So I turn to food for comfort, and to get a break from my uncomfortable feelings.

[Later in the day]

A small part of me wants to stop being the "good little girl." I resist. I stay faithful to the old message that says, "Do what's expected of you. That's the only way you'll survive."

When I ignore that voice — that craving for me to be me — I feel empty. I feel like this especially in relationships — I pretend to agree with my partner (I'm afraid he'll get mad if I disagree) or I blame myself for any difficulties in our relating.

This pattern of fear and isolation started when I was a child. I looked pretty — and that impressed people. But no one really cared how I felt. (That's how I perceived it, anyway.) This made me feel so isolated. (Food was my only friend.)

I did get praise and approval (still do) — because I presented a pleasing image to the world. But it came at a price (still does). To gain acceptance, I ignore my feelings.

I know it is possible to stop pretending to be someone who I'm not.

And to stop stuffing my feelings with food.

How... or when? Not sure.

[Just before going to bed]

Moments ago, I started paying attention to that little voice inside me that's starving for my attention and love. As I do that, the child within me (that part of me which is used to feeling like an emotional orphan) starts to feel a little safer and a little more content.

Right now, I feel more positive about myself and life.

SELF HELP SUGGESTIONS

Nurture the inner child

It is possible to erase the negative messages we adopted when we were young.

It is possible to feel so strong that we don't need addictive substance to cope.

Even though our parents did the best they could, that doesn't mean they gave us what we needed.

Now, as adults, we need to take over... and replace negative self-perceptions with a wholesome, confident self-image.

Visualize

Picture a rainbow above your head.

Breathe in all the vibrant colors of its rays.

Imagine that each ray is nourishing you... and soothing you.

You may still feel connected to the negative messages that you adopted long ago. But you can now weave the nourishment of this rainbow into your thoughts about yourself.

Allow your thoughts to be bathed in these rich, rainbow colors.

Then, visualize the richness of these rays emanating from yourself... from your golden, loving essence... your inner strength.

Fill yourself up with the brightness of your loving essence.

This is your source of power.

This is who you truly are.

This is you — without relying on an addictive substance to cope.

This is you — strong, capable, confident.

This is who you truly are.

DECEMBER 24

*So Busy Helping Others
Neglecting Myself*

I give much more to others than to myself. In my world, everyone else comes first. "I must please… I must impress… I need people to like me." Just like when I was a child.

It's exhausting. I give and give, without a break… without replenishing myself.

I feel almost like a car, traveling at 100 miles per hour with very little gas in my tank.

Food is my fuel. Lots of it. But food is only a temporary pacifier.

I still neglect my emotional needs. My inner child is starving for love and attention. She feels neglected and lonely. She wants to play and have fun.

SELF HELP SUGGESTIONS

Compulsive (extreme/excessive) behavior is typically fear-based.

Example. I go out of my way to please people, because I'm so afraid they won't like me.

Try replacing fear with self-love.

"I don't need people to like me. I hope they will, but I like me. That's what matters most."

Affirm

Write your first name in the space below.

In the past, I _____ was helpful to people because I needed their approval. (That is the child I once was, living through me, wanting people to like her.)

Now I do nice things for people because I <u>want</u> to, not because I need them to like me.

I no longer give so much to others that I have no energy for myself.

I am content. My inner child feels safe and loved.

JANUARY 29

Feeling Isolated
Depleted

———

I visualize my inner child standing in front of me. She is hungry for attention.

I imagine receiving this note from her:

Dear Mom,

You have me cooped up inside. Please take me to the park and play with me.

Mom, when you feel so hungry, but you're full from have just eaten a meal, it's me who is hungry — for love and attention.

Please promise me that you'll pay attention to me.

As I continue to pay attention to how I'm feeling (acknowledge my inner child), I realize that I'm still doing things to gain approval.

When I do that, it's like I'm suffocating my inner child — instead of paying attention to her needs … and loving her.

I still give, give, give to others and do, do, do — but I don't rejuvenate or refill myself.

My only refill is food.

But that's not the refill I need. I need love. The child within me is starving for hugs and companionship, not carbohydrates.

Self Help Suggestion

A reminder of the inner child

This exercise uses a soft, stuffed animal.

Hug this little, stuffed animal at least twice a day, as if it were a little child.

Pay attention to how you feel while you're doing this.

Let this be a visual and tactile reminder of the presence of your inner child who needs you to fill a deep inner void — created by years and years of feeling unloved.

Embrace your loving essence, and say to your inner child, "I love you."

A reminder to practice self-care daily.

Each day, do at least one nurturing activity for yourself.

Affirm

Fill in the blank with your first name and a nurturing statement.

Today, I _____ am _____

_____

_____

Example:

Today, I _____ am setting aside fifteen minutes to relax and spend time with myself.

FEBRUARY 10

*"Making" Things Happen
Approval-Seeking
Inadequacy*

I feel compelled to "make" things happen. I don't trust that things will unfold in a good way.

I'm still hooked on getting people's approval. Today, I undermined myself and ignored my desires — all for approval. I agreed to help a colleague because I felt guilty… I felt like I "should" help out, like I "have to" assist.

But something doesn't feel good about helping for these reasons… like I'm living a lie. This is eating at me. When I agreed to help my colleague, I felt like I had sold my soul…

[Later in the day]

I just came back from helping my colleague.

While I was there, I found myself thinking, "I really don't want to be doing this!"

Then, true to form, I agreed to help her the following week, again.

Driving home, I felt overwhelmed. "How am I going to get out of doing this again?"

When I got home, I binged — cookies and soda to numb the overwhelm.

[Before going to bed]

Insight: I'm realizing how foreign it feels to let life unfold. I'm so afraid that nothing will work out unless I "make" it happen. ("I have to help out my colleague, even if I don't want to. Otherwise she may not like me or want to help me, if I'm in need.")

This is insightful. I've never really looked at this "gotta make it happen" pattern of mine before — and how it is linked to my feelings of inadequacy.

SELF HELP SUGGESTION

Observe and reflect

Do you commit to doing some things for the wrong reasons? Reasons that don't reflect your values?

When we do that, we rip away our inner home by denying our true selves.

And when we deny our true self, invariably we do compulsive things.

It's time to make choices for the right reasons… choices that reflect our values.

Your essence is love.

Let love (not fear/inadequacy) guide your choices.

Let love show you the direction that's best for you.

Promise yourself that from now on you will create experiences for yourself that are comfortable and supportive … experiences that are fueled by love.

MARCH 4

*Guilt Feelings
Low Self-Esteem*

Today it was hard to stand up for myself. I was afraid that people wouldn't respect me.

In the end, I found the courage to do it.

But then I criticized and nagged myself for speaking up: "Why did I? How could I? What is it with me?"

I was consumed with guilt for making this "mistake."

My self-saboteur dug in: "Other people are more confident than you... more at ease than you. They handle challenges better than you. You need them to help you be successful."

I was so preoccupied with self-criticism that I couldn't focus on what I needed to do.

Then this afternoon, a colleague was so nice to me that I felt indebted to her. A few hours later, she asked me a favor. I felt obligated to help her (otherwise, I'd feel guilty).

(Today at work, I raided the vending machine a few times. I needed some sweetness to sugarcoat my bitter feelings.)

[Later today . . .]

Feeling Worthwhile; Independent; Self-Reliant

I'm sensing a shift in how I'm feeling in a good way. I'm realizing that I have a right to assert myself.

I'm realizing that I can treat myself with the same love and respect that I would show to someone I care about... and that I'm not indebted to anyone.

Liking myself gives me courage. I feel more deserving of self-respect.

This sense of self-worth strengthens me. It's a bit easier to not overeat.

I no longer need to stuff myself with food, suppressing my emotions.

I feel more confident. No one can make me feel inferior without my consent.

SELF HELP SUGGESTION

We owe it to ourselves to take the very best care of ourselves.

This includes asserting ourselves, respecting ourselves, and not stuffing down our emotions inside.

Affirm

I _____ give myself permission to assert myself, respect myself, and to make mistakes!

I _____ deserve to be treated well by other people.

I deserve their respect without needing to give anything in return.

I _____ deserve to feel my feelings, and not stuff them down with food (or another "drug of choice"). **My feelings can teach me about myself. My feelings can help me grow**.

MARCH 23

Addictive Behavior — a Way of Coping With Anxiety

I have a big exam tomorrow. Lots of studying today.

And lots of overwhelmed, anxious feelings. "How am I going to memorize all of this in time for the exam?... What if I don't know enough to pass?"

The more I think about the exam, the more panicked I feel. Terrified. So much doubt and worry.

I head for the refrigerator. "I've got to calm down. A slice of cheesecake might help... just one more scoop of ice cream and then I'll study again."

[A few hours later...]

After Binging

All that food didn't give me strength to handle the exam. It made things worse. "I feel so bad about overeating. I'm caught up in the vicious cycle of compulsive behavior. I feel even more anxious and stressed. I'm depressed. This must be rock bottom."

SELF HELP SUGGESTIONS

Reacting to challenges by turning to an addictive substance is a dead-end street. Efforts to pacify self-doubt, struggles and fears with an addictive substance are futile.

It's time to stop looking for strength in all the wrong places. It's time to turn inward.

These questions can begin to set that process in motion.

Am I willing to get really honest with myself?

Am I willing to replace self-doubt with self-trust?

Am I willing to look within for strength, instead of outside of myself?

It's time to let the love that is inside each and every one of us boost our self-esteem.

Self-love radiates a feeling of peace that is sweeter than any candy bar in the universe!

Affirm:

I _____ am no longer willing to let addictive behavior consume all of my energy so that little else can be accomplished.

I _____ am willing to let go of being caught up in the obsessive cycles of addictive behavior.

I _____ no longer need to react to a problem by behaving compulsively.

I _____ can handle all challenges with love.

The Cover-Up.

Compulsive behavior covers up a deeper, inner need.

Recall a time when you were compulsive. What emotion were you covering up?

Example: When I ate cheesecake before my big exam, I was covering up anxiety.

The answer is linked to the child we once were… who talks to us through our emotions.

Ask Yourself:

What am I feeling?

Example:.

How old is the part of me that is feeling this way?

Example: Six years old.

What does that part of me need?

Example: Reassurance that everything will be alright.

Attend to those needs, right now.

Example: I love you. I am here to help you. You are not alone. Everything will be alright.

APRIL 18

*Compulsive Behavior
Addictive Substances and
Relationships*

When I'm heavy into my addiction, my compulsiveness blocks out what I'm feeling.

I need to understand my feelings. It's the only way I can grow.

Today, I'm taking a hard look at my compulsive behavior in relationships. I'm trying to understand why I'm compulsive. I'm trying to figure out how I can behave more positively.

I must slow down before I make decisions about my relationships. I react impulsively, out of need, not strength. My reactivity comes from my needy, inner child — the part of me who is craving love and attention.

I need to nurture this needy part of me. If I don't, my relationships don't stand a chance to be healthy.

When I ignore my neediness, my craving for love causes me to attract addictive relationships.

[Later that day]

I'm realizing that I can take care of myself — whether I'm in a relationship or not.

And if I'm in an unhealthy relationship that I should leave... then I must leave. I have stayed in too many unhealthy relationships because I was afraid to be alone, or afraid that my leaving might hurt the other person. These are not good reasons to stay.

It's becoming clear to me that all my relationships start with me... and that relationships cannot do my "growing" for me...

SELF HELP SUGGESTIONS

The best relationships are those in which **both people feel good about themselves** — neither of them is looking to the relationship to fill an emotional void.

Affirmations to help break relationship addictions.

I _____ can live without him (or her). I am able to rely on myself.

I _____ used to feel uncomfortable about being alone. Now I remind myself that I am never truly alone. I am always connected to my essence — which is love.

This is an excerpt from a letter written from one partner to another — a beautiful example of a loving relationship.

I miss you so much... my missing you goes so beyond romantic love, to such a deep-rooted spiritual connection that you can only be a goddess in my life... for you are so precious to me.

MAY 10

Need for Approval
Emotional Roller Coaster

I am so afraid of failure and rejection. So I'm always trying to be helpful to other people — I want their approval.

I'm so emotional… and so sensitive to how other people treat me. I feel crushed if someone is negative towards me.

I'm on an emotional roller coaster — one moment I feel so high… the next moment, I feel so down. It's exhausting. I long for peace.

Even though I try to get people to like me, I feel lonely. That's how my inner child feels. I've neglected her for so long because I've been paying attention to other things. She longs to be loved.

My perception of myself is so skewed… I feel like a failure. But in reality, I'm successful.

No wonder I eat to escape these painful thoughts and feelings.

Thought for the day: Our thoughts and feelings can lift us up or destroy us.

SELF HELP SUGGESTIONS

Unhealthy fear causes us to feel negatively about ourselves.

Unhealthy fear separates us from our loving selves.

At times, the fear is so intolerable that we numb it out with a compulsive behavior.

Stop the compulsion now.

Stop fear now.

A good place to begin: Reflect on the role that fear plays in your life.

Has fear been a reason for your actions?

Write down your reflections:

_____

_____

_____

_____

_____

_____

How much influence does fear have over what you do?

Write down your reflections:

_____

_____

_____

_____

_____

_____

Many people have a fear of the unknown. Do you?

Write down your reflections:

_____

_____

_____

_____

_____

_____

Reflect and release

This exercise takes place at the ocean. It can strengthen our connection with our loving essence and calm our emotions — so that we can **replace unhealthy fear with strength.**

If you can't actually get to the ocean, imagine yourself being there.

As you visualize yourself by the ocean, or if you are actually sitting alongside the water, watch the movement of the waves and listen to the sounds.

Notice the salty aroma and the spray as the waves break.

See the ocean as a wise, comforting friend — **someone who listens, without judgment or criticism, accepting and patient**.

Use the ocean as a sounding board, releasing all of your fears and worries. Trust that the trusted ocean will wash it all away.

Let the rhythmic motion of the water calm you and soothe you.

Embrace this tranquil feeling.

Let this serenity be part of your day today…. and every day.

JUNE 11

Suppressing Emotions
Failure
Abandonment
Emotional Roller Coaster

I recently ended a relationship. I feel like a failure, abandoned. I'm petrified of being alone.

I don't know if I can make it through the day…

I can't sleep, exercise or concentrate — I can't do anything.

I'm trying to keep busy to avoid feeling this aloneness.

I rationalize my feelings ("It wasn't meant to be… you're better off without that loser…")

I stuff my lonely feelings with food — I'll do anything not to feel this hurt.

[Later the same day…]

Facing the Fear…

I need to face my fears. It's the only way that they can be released.

Ending this relationship means releasing many fears. I need to take time to heal.

Right now…

[Before going to bed]

Letting the Fear Surface…

I'm letting my fear surface. I feel anxious, vulnerable…

I feel tender and sensitive.

I need to keep facing this fear, or it will continue to run my life.

SELF HELP SUGGESTIONS

Fear is often at the root of compulsive behavior.

You deserve to be free of fear.

You deserve to no longer behave compulsively.

Meditation

Close your eyes.

Inhale deeply.

Exhale and relax.

Again…

Inhale… breathing in strength.

Exhale… letting go of fear.

Now shift your focus to your heart.

Imagine your heart is filled with your favorite color. A healing color.

Now imagine your heart is glowing…

And this glow radiates throughout your body.

You are pure love. There is no space in your existence for fear.

Now that you are connected to your loving essence, affirm:

"I have nothing to fear. There is nothing I can't handle. Everything I need is within me."

Enjoy the peace that you feel right now. Enjoy feeling safe. **Enjoy the love.**

When you're ready, gently open your eyes and adjust to the light in your environment.

CHAPTER TWO

Learning To Heal

JULY 1

Taking Action
Freedom From Fear

―――――

I'm facing my fears. Sometimes I want to turn back, look the other way.

But letting go of fear makes room for self-love… I feel so at home with that feeling.

I want more of it.

I want to be free of self-defeating, emotional games.

I want to be free of fear.

Many of my fears are about the future. Instead of living in the now, my mind leaps ahead, worrying about tomorrow. My fear of living caused me to seek refuge in food.

I have choices — I can stay locked in these fearful thoughts, or I can heal them.

I choose to heal them.

[*Later in the day*]

I just spent a few moments breathing and visualizing inhaling love from the top of my head, letting it travel down to the bottom of my feet.

That felt so good. I don't want to give away my power again — relying on food for comfort. And I don't want to depend on other people for approval.

I am beginning to have a sense of how strong we all are.

Deep breathing is so calming. I feel quite nourished and relaxed... but also light and energetic.

My emotions are more balanced. I feel more in touch with my loving self. Grateful.

SELF HELP SUGGESTIONS

Visualize

Picture yourself standing inside a large balloon.

This balloon is filled with love — the love and strength of your true essence.

Tell yourself that you can access your own power from this source, at all times.

Now focus on the area on the top of your head.

Breathe this love into that area.

Imagine the love flowing through your whole body… like a soft mist bathing you.

Commit to staying in this presence. This belongs to you. Nobody can take it from you.

Realize that you never totally left your true essence. You are rediscovering it.

But it is your responsibility to let every choice emanate from love, not from fear.

Keep breathing in love… as if it is a brilliant laser beam radiating throughout your being.

Affirm

I _____ honor my right to make choices fueled by love.

I _____ feel loving and loved.

JULY 8

No Reason To Feel Guilty

Many children learn negative messages about themselves that they carry into adulthood.

As a child, I felt that everything I did was wrong. I doubted everything I did. It was a lonely existence. I tried to comfort myself with food. Hours of binging. . . then self-hatred and guilt for what I had put my body through.

As an adult, I still sometimes have guilt-attacks — like when I "fall off the wagon" as I'm finding my way back to self-love.

Guilt is brutal.

I'm realizing that I have nothing to feel guilty about.

And that when I feel guilty, it's a carryover from childhood.

As I nurture my inner child with love, my guilt disappears.

SELF HELP SUGGESTIONS

Nurturing the inner child

Today, I reflected on guilt and wrote down these thoughts:

You have a right to grow and reach your highest potential.

You do not owe anyone anything.

You deserve to feel worthy.

You are worthy.

As a child, you lived with so much guilt.

Say out loud to your inner child:

"I'm sorry you felt guilty. That was unfair. You did nothing wrong. I'm your parent now and I love you. You can have fun and play now. I won't abandon you."

Once our wounded, inner child feels heard and understood, guilt tends to dissipate.

[Later today]

I Sat Down To Write Again. These Words Poured Out of Me.

Many children don't get enough emotional nurturance. This can cause them to feel inadequate, fearful and self-critical.

These feelings tend to carry over into adulthood.

As adults they may consciously or unconsciously, conceal this negativity by getting a good job and/or raising a family, etc. — giving the "appearance" of being successful.

But at some point, the vacuum created during childhood invariably resurfaces.

Then the absence of love is very obvious (the adult might develop a full-blown addiction, for example — seeking love and comfort, through food or compulsive shopping).

Visualize

Reflect on the erroneous messages you adopted during your childhood.

Have compassion for the guilt, doubt, and fear that you felt because of these messages.

Breathe love into these negative feelings.

Only then can the child within begin to heal.

AUGUST 24

Releasing Dependent Relationships

As children, many of us had role models who were emotionally needy.

To fulfill their own needs, they made us dependent on them — by controlling us and overprotecting us, for example.

As adults, we may attract similar dependent-type relationships.

When we realize that these relationships are unhealthy, we're afraid to leave… we feel dependent (just like we did as children).

And we feel guilty for wanting to leave. We feel selfish for even thinking about leaving… and not catering to the relationship.

[After dinner]

I am managing my life well. I don't need to depend on people to cope.

The sense of security that I felt as a child (and as an adult) in dependent relationships with overprotective, controlling caregivers (and partners) is not "real" security.

I am focusing on severing my connection to the dependent relating that I experienced as a child, and continue to engage in as an adult.

SELF HELP SUGGESTIONS

Are you in a dependent relationship?

Ask yourself:

"What is expected of me in this relationship?"

"What price am I paying for staying in this relationship?"

Visualize

Reflect on a relationship in your life that needs healing.

Imagine that this relationship has a price tag attached to it.

What is the message on this price tag? Are you paying a price for being in this relationship?

Send love to the message on the price tag, and release it. It is a script from long ago that is no longer serving you.

Affirm

I _____ love myself and I can take care of myself.

I _____ am strong and secure.

SEPTEMBER 1

Self-Appreciation
Self-Respect

Ugh, my body's gross — stomach too big, chest too small. So much is wrong with me!

I can't stand all this self-hate. I need to numb out with food.

I feel so stupid ("Why did you say that! People will think you're stupid... Don't you have anything better to say!"). I don't want to feel so inept, so I numb out with food.

OMG, I'm so inadequate! I hate feeling this way. I need to distract myself with food.

[Later in the afternoon]

I have grown a lot. I know that my feelings of inadequacy don't mean I've regressed. They're from a deeper layer of insecurity that I get to clear out. I am grateful for that.

I want to appreciate and respect myself more. I feel committed to replacing negative self-talk with gentle, loving truths about myself.

[Around dusk]

I just had a beautiful walk by the ocean. My self-critical thoughts were in high-gear, but as soon as I heard them I tossed them in the ocean. This felt liberating. Thank you, Mother Nature, for partnering with me as I heal. I'm inspired.

Alone-time is important. I commit to carving out time each day to be with myself.

I am enjoying sharing these messages with myself to amp up my self-worth:

— *You have a beautiful, healthy body and an intelligent, creative mind.*

— *You have every right to express yourself, totally and completely.*

— *You deserve to enjoy fun and pleasure.*

— *You have so many beautiful qualities.*

SELF HELP SUGGESTIONS

Visualize

Close your eyes and picture an image of yourself.

Take a few deep breaths as you lovingly appreciate what you see.

Let go of any negative perceptions. Dismiss them from your mind.

Think about your goals and desires.

Become clear about what you want to achieve.

You deserve to be successful.

Keep reflecting on your goals for a few moments…

Now visualize them in your mind.

Shower these images with love.

Appreciate yourself. Respect yourself.

Affirm

Life is an adventure as I _____ passionately pursue my goals.

The world is my playground as I _____ release worry and doubt.

With humility, I _____ am in awe of all that I am, and so grateful.

OCTOBER 20

Saying "Yes" to Relaxation and Play

Each person has a little girl or a little boy within — the child we once were, who lives on inside of us, through our feelings. We need to allow the little girl or boy to play.

My inner child is happy when I'm in a relationship — she enjoys playing with my partner's inner child.

As kids, boys are encouraged to play. That's one reason why the little boy in the man is usually playful, and why men have many play-toys — they were taught how to be little boys.

Little girls aren't taught how to really play… things get serious and they're taught to play grown-up games. They're given baby dolls as practice for the real babies when they grow up.

I need to treasure and nurture my delightful, childlike qualities.

I'm grateful to my inner child. She can be so joyful. I love spending time with her.

Life has not been easy for her. Yet she's still so beautifully alive. I am so proud of her.

SELF HELP SUGGESTIONS

Affirm

I _____ delight in the joy of my inner child.

I _____ am having fun having fun.

Create a list of interesting activities that you enjoy.

Commit to setting aside time to do fun things with your inner child. This will be playtime.

Invite other adults to come along, encouraging their inner children to play as well.

OCTOBER 30

The Rewards of Change and Growth

I've been making big changes. I'm feeling a huge shift as I replace fear with love.

These changes can be unsettling, but it's also exciting to return "home" to my "self."

I'm letting go of self-destructive behaviors.

There are some areas of my life that I still need to change. I don't know how, yet.

"Not knowing" is OK. It often happens when we let go of the "old" (familiar) to make room for the "new" (unfamiliar).

[Later in the day]

I feel confused. I am reevaluating my beliefs and goals.

I am questioning things deeply:

Where am I going in life? What do I really want?

I am considering:

Who am I? How well do I know myself?

I am assessing my involvement in some situations, and asking myself:

Is this of value to me?

This is a big adjustment. I've never really asked myself these questions before.

In the past, I had firm ideas of what I should be doing. I never consulted my inner self, as I'm now beginning to do.

With this change comes an empty feeling.

This emptiness has existed since childhood. I'm realizing why I stayed busy and compulsive — anything to avoid feeling this emptiness.

Extra gentle, but firm reminder to self:

Have the courage to face this emptiness — without judgment, guilt or blame. It's the only way you will grow.

You are not alone. Love is walking with you through this emptiness… as you return back home to self-love.

[Later that day]

I'm realizing that the way I did things in the past totally didn't support my true needs.

Even though I have achieved success (professionally, socially, personally) a little voice inside keeps saying, "Stop living this lie. Live your truth."

As I pay attention to that voice, I visualize wonderful things unfolding in the future — situations and opportunities that are in synch with my true self.

I don't want to feel obligated to anyone or locked into anything anymore.

I'm realizing that I can choose what is best for me. That feels fantastic.

SELF HELP SUGGESTIONS

Need to do some reevaluating about your life?

These questions can be a good start:

Who am I?

How well do I know myself?

What matters to me?

Are there some areas of my life that I want to change?

How can I make this happen?

Be kind to yourself as you reflect. That means no self judgment, guilt, fault or blame.

Write down your reflections.

_____

_____

_____

_____

_____

NOVEMBER 29

Making Anger Work for Us

I used to be afraid to express my anger ("People will take it personally and not like me.") So I became meek and quiet.

I know now that not all anger is bad.

Constructive anger helps me to assert myself and say, "No, thank you," "No, I don't want that," "No, that doesn't work for me."

Destructive anger happens when we react out of proportion to a situation — when people yell, throw things, break things, and/or are violent.

Destructive anger happens when we stuff down our constructive anger… and we let all this anger build up, until there's no room to hold any more anger inside. And then we explode.

I know now that when I say to someone, "Please don't do that," it's not personal. I'm talking about their behavior, not them.

[Later in the day]

More Writing...

I just talked with my landlord about renewing my lease. He is being unreasonable.

My old self: "Accept his offer or he may dump you as a tenant," (fear of rejection).

My stronger, healthier self: "No, his terms are unreasonable. I need to speak up." (Later, I spoke up. I got what I wanted, and... he didn't "dump" me.)

Although not all of my "assertive efforts" have happy endings, it doesn't feel right anymore to swallow my feelings and be a doormat.

For as long as I can remember, I suppressed my emotions. As a child, I ate compulsively to suppress painful, angry feelings. But food didn't erase my feelings.

My inner child used to be buried underneath my suppressed anger. I am learning to pay attention to her.

Sometimes my feelings are so strong that it's not wise for me to talk with anyone at that moment. I'd probably say things that I wish I could then take back.

So I buy time and set my feelings aside, or I release them safely by pounding a pillow, using a hand towel with a knot tied on one end.

SELF HELP SUGGESTION

Have the courage to face feelings like anger and pain, safely.

Affirm

One of the most precious gifts that I _____ can give myself is to appropriately and safely express how I feel, and not numb out with an addictive substance or behavior.

DECEMBER 12

Love Has Set Me Free

―――――

I feel strong. It's a good place to be.

I have worked hard to reach this strength. I have love to thank for this.

Love helped me get here.

Love helped me to trust myself and to feel free!

Negative self-talk resurfaces now and then. But I quickly dispel those cruel untruths.

I am beginning to feel relaxed and peaceful, more consistently.

I set aside quiet time every day to savor feeling so at ease.

Serenity is sweet.

SELF HELP SUGGESTIONS

Affirm

I _____ feel content and secure.

Repeat this affirmation at the same time every day, for seven to ten days.

Visualize

Picture a screen door between your inner world and the outer world.

Your inner world reflects beauty, love and joy.

This screen door is like a filter, protecting you from negativity in your environment.

Keep the door closed. Let this filter protect you.

Only allow positive qualities to enter.

Talk and relate through the screen.

From now on, keep everything outside the screen until you know that it matches what you want to experience — warm feelings, serenity and strength.

Thought for the day: **I no longer need to say "Yes" to everything.**

CHAPTER THREE

Living With Love

JANUARY 2

Self-Reliance, Freedom From Addictions

I am learning to depend on myself. I make room in my life for quiet time to tune in to my essence — to love. (Such a contrast to my hectic, on-the-go schedule of the past.)

The more I get to know myself, the more empathy I have for how hard I used to be on myself and how frightened I used to feel.

I felt panicked all the time (working on too many projects at once, frantically trying to meet other people's deadlines). To cope with the panic, I ate.

I pretended to be in control, but I felt totally out of control.

I was sure no one could help and that I had to fix my problems on my own. People did care, but I rejected their concern. I did cry out for help — when no one could hear.

It is wonderful to write about this inner warfare as an experience of the past.

Today, I reclaim my true essence. Now my choices flow from love. This is how I have released myself from the brutal grip of my addictions.

SELF HELP SUGGESTIONS

Breathe

Inhale, to the count of four.

Exhale, to the count of four.

As you inhale, think of inhaling power.

As you exhale, breathe out satisfaction.

Repeat.

Inhale, to the count of four.

Exhale, to the count of four.

As you inhale, breathe in power.

As you exhale, breathe out satisfaction.

You are beginning to feel your power and strength.

You are feeling more calm and self-accepting.

You no longer compromise yourself to please others.

Be proud of your commitment to growth — to live a life fueled by love, not fear.

FEBRUARY 3

*Loving Myself Makes Me Love the World
And the World Loves Me Back*

As I grow stronger and everything I do is infused with love, it seems like the world is loving me back — when I smile at someone, then they smile back at me.

Life is beginning to flow.

There are challenges. And there are upsets and disappointments. But I take them in stride and safely release my emotions if I need to (example: pound a pillow — to release anger — with a hand towel that has a knot tied on one end).

Stress doesn't unnerve me anymore — I know there is nothing I can't handle or somehow overcome. I know now that self-love can get me through life's rough spots.

I'm grateful for the opportunities that have created space for me to grow and love.

MARCH 15

For the Love of Self, Reparenting

My inner child feels vulnerable. I haven't been suppressing this little person with food — so she feels unprotected.

She feels reassured when I tell her,

"I'm your parent now. You're safe, protected and loved."

I am grateful to my biological parents for raising me the best way they knew how.

But much of my growth is because I've learned how to be my own parent.

Self-love fills the void I felt as a child. My inner child is happy. She feels safe to say,

"Wow, finally you're paying attention to me. I have wanted this for so long."

Today I am overflowing with the love from myself to myself, and for others.

I am giving myself a gift — of love. This feels amazing.

APRIL 1

Addictions = Abandoned

I feel very connected to myself. My choices are no longer based on what I should do. Now it's about what I want to do.

I was an addict for so long. It feels good to finally rely on myself (not a substance).

It feels wonderful to appreciate myself.

It feels wonderful to know that my beautiful life is powered by love.

I love being with myself and with other people who are also excited about their lives. Negativity is no longer my reality.

I have released my addictions. I am learning from past mistakes. I could have remained in the destructive, addictive process, but instead I chose healing.

The big lesson?

No one keeps me deluded — except myself.

I can be my strongest enemy. I can also be my own greatest friend.

SELF HELP SUGGESTION

Visualize

Picture yourself saying goodbye to your addictions, insecurities and negativity.

Breathe strength into this image.

From the deep core of love within, tell yourself:

"You are wonderful.

You can be successful.

You can flourish.

I support you in being your best self.

I am your support (not some substance or compulsion).

I can help you. Reach out to me, I am here."

MAY 5

Support and Encouragement

Change is the end phase of growth.

The first phase of change in my addictions journey was my dissatisfaction with myself (an aching, inner void that needed to be filled — but not with an addictive substance).

The second phase in the change process was my decision to fill this inner void.

The third phase was reflected in the steps I took to make the change.

This three phase process to transform a problem into a solution, takes time.

I've had to remind myself, often:

"Be patient and open-minded while you're changing and growing.

Don't be discouraged.

The quest to become the best, most loving, content person you can be, is your own personal challenge and at times the journey back home can be lonely and demanding."

There were times when I felt totally alone, hopeless and helpless. I'm so glad I reached out to trusted people for support — their encouragement helped me stay on track.

I recognize the value of support and caring from people in my life — especially during challenging times. I am also committed to being my own best friend, always.

SELF HELP SUGGESTION

Affirm

I _____ am confident that everything I am experiencing is leading me back home to myself.

JUNE 1

Listening to my Intuition
Releasing Child-Like Reactions

Today I recognize my progress. I'm filled with self-respect and appreciation.

But from time to time, I slip into old, negative thinking patterns.

I'm pleased that I don't criticize myself anymore for having these thoughts and that I don't think of this "slip" as regression.

Instead, I try to understand why these thinking patterns reemerged. I ask myself:

"What is the lesson in this for me? (Be kinder to myself? Be more patient?)"

Then I forgive myself for taking a few steps back… and move on.

The more I pay attention to my intuition and care for my inner child, the happier I feel. When my emotions (inner child) are calm and I am guided by my intuition, I feel free.

This is such a contrast to how I felt as a young adult — as if I were in a jail, imprisoned by the consequences of destructive childhood experiences.

I am touched by how much emotional hurt has been cleared. I've released many of the immature, emotional reactions which colored much of my adult life.

I now know that there is no person, place or substance in the world to which I can flee, to escape myself and how I feel.

Loving myself is the way to return home.

SELF HELP SUGGESTIONS

Visualize

Picture your inner child in front of you.

Embrace this precious little being with loving hugs.

Ask your inner child to forgive you for not being the best parent for him or her.

Promise that child that you will be _____ (example: kinder) and more _____ (example: patient).

JULY 10

I'm Not a Slave to my Addictions

My darkened, emotional world of childhood left me feeling empty, wounded, and hurt.

To fill this inner void, I compulsively devoured food. Over and over.

For a long time, food was my primary relationship.

For a long time, I was unhappy. I blamed my traumatic past for that.

No longer.

Now, powered by love, I take responsibility for my wellbeing. I prioritize replacing bad habits with healthier ones.

The painful, addictive cycle is not a disease that I am stuck with. I am learning simple, practical ways to transform destructive behavior into actions that are powered by love.

Today, my disease process is reversed.

Today, I am learning to unlock my potential and live from my heart — from love.

Today, I am filled with hope and inspiration.

SELF HELP SUGGESTION

Affirm

Today, I _____ am making empowering choices.

Today, I _____ find happiness from within myself.

Today, I _____ am able to give and receive love.

AUGUST 8

Easy Does It

I keep hearing these words in my mind, today:

"You have a choice about how you live your life. You can choose to live in the solution, or you can continue to wallow in the problem."

I choose the solution. No more living without love.

My motto for today?

"Easy does it."

I feel so wonderfully calm. And my visualizations and safe, emotional catharsis (I've been doing quite a bit of pillow-pounding with a knotted towel, and pillow-screaming [releasing fear by screaming into a pillow- to muffle the sound], together with a deepening self-awareness, are dissolving the bitterness, regret, and loneliness I used to feel.

As I continue to heal, my confidence is growing. It's as if "all's right with the world," no matter what. Love rules!

SELF HELP SUGGESTION

Each morning when you wake up, spend a few moments with your inner child.

One way to do this, is to grab a throw pillow (or your soft, stuffed animal).

Then close your eyes and hold the pillow, as if you're holding the child you once were.

Pay attention to what you are feeling (i.e., pay attention to your inner child).

Pay attention to whether there is anything that you need, emotionally (example: understanding, support, comfort, reassurance, company, or empathy).

Give that to yourself, right now.

(Example: "I understand that you're afraid of that big dog. You're safe, I won't let the dog harm you.")

Soothe and support your precious self.

Enjoy healing your fears from the past, with love.

SEPTEMBER 19

Facing Feelings Head-on

Some angry feelings bubbled up, today. I was tempted to not face them. But I'm so glad I pounded the pillow, and screamed into it — that helped, a lot.

The relief I felt reminded me of the many years that I avoided facing my feelings. I just wallowed in self-pity and I felt victimized by life.

I remember learning — the hard way — that unless I face my feelings, healing can't happen.

Things came to a head one day, when I "got" it — all those years spent blaming my myself and others for my despairing life, had been a huge waste of time. No benefit at all!

This awareness was a turning point. It was time to deal with reality and begin to heal.

I'm grateful for what I learned from that awareness — how necessary it is to be honest with oneself. The fact that I'd wasted all those years avoiding myself, drove the point home.

And I'm grateful that from that point on, I found the courage to face my feelings. And underneath those scared, hurt, angry feelings, I found love... self-love.

I'm grateful that I faced my feelings today — and discharged them safely, instead of avoiding them and stuffing them down with food. Self-defeating behavior is a choice. No more of that!

SELF HELP SUGGESTIONS

Visualize

Picture yourself in one of your favorite places (at the beach, hiking, hanging out at home, etc.).

You are relaxed and comfortable.

See yourself releasing the negative feelings that you've been living with for so long.

See that negativity transforming into a glowing ball of light and merging with the sun.

Forgive yourself for holding onto that negativity for so long.

Now see yourself for who you truly are — love.

See that love radiating through you — from the top of your head to the tips of your toes.

Feel it. Be it. Own it.

Affirm

I love you _____ and I forgive you for _____
_____.

I'm proud of you and I believe in you.

OCTOBER 2

As Love Grows Within
Abundance Is Reflected in my Actions…
Facing Feelings Head-on

Now that I've chosen self-love, I relate to the world differently (with love, not fear).

In the past, life was scary, lonely, and empty… now, life is becoming fun, exciting, and full.

My growth impacts everything I do, delightfully.

For this, I am so grateful.

I have come home!

SELF HELP SUGGESTIONS

This meditation can nourish and soothe our nervous system and emotions.

Set aside some alone time to reflect, preferably in or close to nature (at a park, a garden, or any setting with trees).

If it is not possible to be near a tree, then imagine you are near one.

Sit down (or imagine you're sitting down) with your back to the tree. As your spine touches the tree, allow yourself to feel nourished and protected.

Inhale, breathing in nourishment.

Exhale, feeling protected.

Now imagine that you are surrounded by a big, shimmering bubble.

This bubble is filled with love — a love that emanates from you… from your essence.

Inhale, breathing in this love.

Exhale, feeling that you are this love.

Spend a few moments feeling the love… recognizing that you are this love.

As you connect with your loving essence in this way, you realize that **nothing can negatively affect your inner home — it is invincible, dependable, and eternal.**

NOVEMBER 2

With Love at our Side, We Don't Fear the Unknown

I feel a bit shaky today. I know that this is part of the recovery process — the more that I release old crutches and patterns, the more there'll be times where I feel a bit chaotic.

Like now. I feel like I have one foot on a boat and the other foot on a raft. But I don't quite know where the raft is headed. So it's feels like I'm taking a big risk.

[Later in the day]

I'm feeling stronger.

That feeling of being "adrift" that I felt earlier today, has passed.

In the past, when I felt this way, I received support from friends, teachers, and others who had travelled a similar path to heal their addictions.

Right now, I feel strong enough to support myself.

That is empowering.

DECEMBER 15

Welcome Home — Goodbye Negativity

Just came home from having dinner with friends. So great to be able to eat moderately, instead of being in binge-mode (those days are so over).

At dinner, a friend asked:

"Do you worry that you're going to 'fall off the wagon' again?"

My answer:

"Nope. Thanks to self-love, there's no reason to be compulsive. I feel so at home and at ease with myself. I'll never trade a love-based life for a fear-driven one."

That said, now and then self-criticism does try to wear me down. It fails though — miserably.

Because now I know that I have a choice — I can believe that harsh criticality and feel depressed about it, or I can stand firm in love.

This is probably one of the most important choices that I'll make in my life.

Thought for the day:

When love is present, negativity doesn't stand a chance.

SELF HELP SUGGESTIONS

Visualize

Send love to any self-critical thoughts, changing self-sabotage into self-appreciation.

As you release this negativity, affirm:

It is time to let go of you. I do not need you anymore.

I am doing this with love. I am not angry at you. I am not rejecting you.

Stay focused on these loving thoughts until the negativity has dissolved and is erased.

Love can now take over.

Love reigns.

FEBRUARY 14

Happy Valentine's Day — Every Day!

———

Love and fear (negativity) cannot coexist.

When we release fear, love blossoms.

Then every day becomes a Valentine's Day.

Now that I've come home to love, my inner child feels welcomed and so comfortable.

Happy Valentine's Day!

Welcome Home.

FEBRUARY 28

Welcome Home

When we trade an addictive lifestyle for a life of love, this is very empowering.

When we come home to love, our inner child is healed, and merges with our adult self — a beautiful union.

When we come home to love, we are powered by wisdom, insight, and support.

When we come home to love, we have access to all the beautiful qualities of "home."

Welcome Home.

PARTING WORDS

When you are struggling with addiction, it can feel hellish and isolating. You might feel extremely lonely, at times, or feel too ashamed to talk about what you're going through. You might feel like there's a void inside of you that can never be filled.

Hopefully, in reading this book, you have come to understand that you selected your "drug of choice" (food, booze, sex, etc.) because you are craving… something. Perhaps you crave comfort, security, excitement, entertainment, attention, love, all of the above, or some other kind of quality or feeling.

Hopefully, you have also come to understand that it is possible to generate these types of feelings for yourself, by yourself, without requiring anything "external" to do it for you.

For example: you can take a deep breath, meditate, visualize a positive scene in your mind, or talk kindly to yourself to create a beautiful feeling of "peacefulness" that emanates from "inside" of you — rather than trying to feel "peaceful" by relying on something that exists "outside" of you, like a bottle of wine or a box of brownies.

This is what it means to be **"emotionally self-reliant"**: relying on yourself to generate the feelings that you yearn to feel. Relying on yourself to soothe yourself, to uplift yourself, to energize yourself, and to successfully meet life's many challenges. As self-reliance grows, addiction tends to subside. It may not happen overnight or in a completely linear way, but if you are willing to patiently "do the personal growth work" to strengthen your emotional self-reliance — like possibly implementing some of the "self-help suggestions" that I share inside this book — it is possible to begin to move away from addiction and towards freedom. I sincerely believe this — and I am especially convinced, after observing many clients over the years, do just this.

Lastly, in reading this book, I hope you have come to realize that you are not alone on your healing journey. There are many people who truly understand what you are going through, people who are working on building more emotional self-reliance, just like you, as well as thousands of trained professionals who would love to help you.

Next up: I've included some resources (written materials, audios, etc.) that may interest you as you continue forward in your healing journey…

RESOURCES...TO CONTINUE THE HEALING JOURNEY

Welcome Home is "technically" complete, but I wanted to give you some more resources on compulsive behaviors, addictive tendencies, self-love, and stress management... as you continue your healing journey.

Here are some that may interest you — articles I've authored,[1] Life Guides I've created, and books I've written, to savor at your leisure.

Enjoy to the fullest ...

ARTICLES

5 Ways to Stop Yourself from Eating When You're not Hungry.
— Originally published on Psych Central.

In addition to believing in yourself and your ability to handle life's challenges without the illusory "help" of food [or whatever person,

---

[1] All articles and links to articles that are included in this section, were published online only.

place, or thing, someone might turn to as a coping mechanism], in this article I also ay out five strategies to consider implementing, in am effort to thwart using food [or any addictive substance/behavior for that matter] to cope.

Strategies include: Identifying the real source of hunger (clue: it's not physical), dialoguing with the food, and remembering the downside of eating for the wrong reasons... disappointment afterwards, and physical discomfort.

https://psychcentral.com/blog/5-ways-to-stop-yourself-from-eating-when-youre-not-hungry/

Learning to Feed A Hungry Heart — Without Binging on Food.
Originally published on MariaShriver.com. Now on Psychology Today.

In this article, I describe how using food to soothe and fill my inner emotional void, brought me nothing but misery.

Then there was a pivotal moment when I got fed-up with feeling miserable, and instead of eating when I wasn't physically hungry, I began to ask myself: "What are you really hungry for, deep down?" It always came back to love.

In time, and with practice, I learned to feed my hungry heart with love, not food. That changed everything.

https://www.psychologytoday.com/intl/blog/all-grown/201904/learning-feed-my-hungry-heart

Stressed Out at Work? How to Cope — Without Turning to Food or Booze.
Originally published on The Huffington Post.

Workplace demands and pressure seems to "come with the territory" in so many instances. It's no surprise then, that many people routinely try to "escape" this stress by consuming something sweet [lots of it! say, a pint of ice cream], numbing out with alcohol, or some other pacifier. A far healthier approach would be to manage work-related stress by relying on one's inner strength. To learn more, including my five stress relief techniques, this article is a must-read.

https://www.huffpost.com/entry/stressed-out-at-work-how_n_6711034

Are You Addicted to Your Job? 7 Ways to Tell
Originally published on The Muse.

In this article, I outline seven questions that readers can ask themselves as part of a mini self-evaluation to understand the reasons behind why they work as hard as they do — so they can determine if they're a workaholic (which typically has fear at its roots, in one form or another).

I also include some a basic self-talk strategy that workaholics can consider implementing, as a first step to breaking the cycle and bringing more balance to their relationship with with their work.

Side note: The Muse is an award-winning online career resource, with over 4 million quality, professional members. I'm honored to have received the praise below, from Adrian Granzella Larssen, Editor-in-Chief, in response to article that I wrote for The Muse:

"Wow! This is fantastic stuff. You're clearly incredible at what you do, and I'm so thrilled to share your advice with our audience!"

https://www.themuse.com/advice/are-you-addicted-to-your-job-7-ways-to-tell?ref=search

Why Accomplishment Often Leaves Us Feeling Empty
Originally published on The Daily Love. Now on Psychology Today.

Would you believe that the best day of my life was also my worst! That was also the day that I became convinced that earning loads of praise (something I was addicted to) is no substitute for feelings of "self-worth".

And if I had any doubts that eating to soothe my inner emotional void leads me to feel even emptier, not better, on that day my doubts were put to rest, permanently.

Curious how to dig oneself out of this agonizing, addictive cycle? I write about that and more, in this article.

http://thedailylove.com/why-accomplishment-often-leaves-us-feeling-empty/

Why I Still Believe People Can Change
Originally published on Positively Positive.

Over the course of decades of working in the field of emotional wellness, I've seen so many people release negative emotions and embrace love. That's why I believe people can change… even someone who stopped dating (fear of rejection), but found the confidence to date again and fell-in-love. Read this article to learn more.

BOOKS (PAPERBACK/KINDLE)

It Starts With You. How To Raise Happy, Successful Children By Being The Best Role Model You Can Possibly Be — A Guidebook, by Dr. Gelb

"What is a parenting book doing in the Resource section of *Welcome Home*, a book that focuses on releasing addictions?" Good question.

For the answer, check out Chapter 20 of It Starts With You. This chapter addresses the question of whether a parent who is struggling with addiction / alcoholism and self-identifies as not being OK, can still be an effective parent for a child. My closing words to this chapter: "Recovery is possible. Progress is possible. Anything is possible."

More specifically, "If your heart is open and you have a real desire to heal — and if you are willing to reach inside yourself and grab on tight to some genuine courage — then anything is possible."

https://www.amazon.com/Starts-You-Successful-Becoming-Guidebook/dp/0692647392/ref=tmm_pap_swatch_0?_encoding=UTF8&qid=1553581148&sr=1-4

The Love Tune-Up: How To Amp Up The Love That's Naturally Inside You to Have Happy, Healthy Relationships — A 14-Day Course That Can Change Your Life

I created The Love Tune-Up because healthy love is the answer to every problem, in one way or another. Everyone has the capacity to find deep reserves of self-love, within. Where there is love, addictions cannot exist.

With this 14-day course, you'll have access to 14 short lessons (and a few more surprises!) to help you tune-up and upgrade your relationship with yourself. Lessons to help you move back into your natural, unburdened state of being — free of guilt, shame or unresolved anger. Lessons on moving back home… into Love.

http://drsuzannegelb.com/love-tune-up-14-day-course/

E-BOOKS

The Life Guides.

I wrote this series of guidebooks to help you successfully navigate some of life's trickiest challenges. Each e-book includes educational information sourced from my 30+ years of coaching and counseling in the field of emotional wellness, exercises to help you release stress, anger, and insecurity, and an audio companion that you can listen to on-the-go. Available here.

http://drsuzannegelb.com/life-guides-by-dr_gelb/

The Life Guide on How To Reach Your Ideal Weight — Through Kindness Not Craziness, can be a relevant companion to *Welcome Home*. When a person's weight yo-yos all over the scale, compulsive overeating (or undereating) tends to be the cause. This addictive tendency invariably has its roots in emotional emptiness, as pointed out in *Welcome Home*.

http://drsuzannegelb.com/life-guide-ideal-weight/

Praise for Dr. Gelb's Life Guides

"Dr. Gelb has a gentle spirit that instantly makes you feel like you've come home. The depth of her wisdom is undeniable, her curiosity is insatiable and her love is palpable. These qualities make her the perfect guide for life. In the pages of the Life Guides you will find practical and proven processes to support you in living your great life. Whether it's heart-centered wisdom on navigating the dating world, love-based strategies for becoming a parent, or reaching your ideal weight through kindness, Dr. Gelb's Life Guides are gifts to be treasured."

— Dr. Gemma Stone, Psychologist, Mentor, Author

"Learning how to love yourself and treat yourself kindly — even when your life, career, body, and relationships aren't 'totally perfect' — is one of the hardest things to do. Dr. Suzanne Gelb breaks down the art of self-love into practical steps. No woo-woo vagueness. Just easy-to-follow exercises pulled from her 28-year career in the field. If you're looking for practicality and effectiveness, these Life Guides are a steal of a deal."

—Susan Hyatt, Master Certified Life Coach, Published Author

"This Life Guide came at the perfect time. My two fears about losing weight were dispelled immediately and it was such a relief to know that I can start looking after myself without the worry of going to the gym or going on another desperate diet.

The audio helped re-frame the reasons why I've let my weight spiral out of control and the work book helped me set out an action plan. Thanks Dr. Gelb for your Life Guide, here's to a happier, healthier life."

—Amanda Herbert, photographer

ABOUT THE AUTHOR

Dr. Suzanne Gelb, PhD, JD is a psychologist, life coach, TV commentator, and author.

Growing up in South Africa under apartheid exposed Suzanne to the darker side of humanity at a very young age.

After struggling with fear and depression for decades, and battling eating disorders, she ultimately learned how to transform her entire life: healing the wounds of the past, forgiving herself and others, and learning to love and respect herself — no matter what.

Today, she lives in the United States, where she runs two thriving practices — coaching and psychotherapy.

Her inspiring insights on personal growth have been featured on more than 200 radio programs, over 200 television interviews, and online at Time, Forbes, Newsweek, The Huffington Post, NBC's Today, Lifehacker, The Daily Love, Positively Positive, Psychology Today, and more.

As a contributing writer to *Psychology Today* where she has her own column, "All Grown Up," Dr. Gelb has written articles that involve addictive behaviors, including, Learning To Feed My Hungry Heart, My Journey from Bingeing to Wholeness and Why Accomplishment Often Leaves Us Feeling "Empty," How to Heal that Longing, At Last. Her powerful article, Stressed Out at Work? How to Cope -- Without Turning to Food or Booze, was published on The Huffington Post.

To learn more visit DrSuzanneGelb.com.

INDEX

A

abandonment, 5, 37
action(s), 34, 44, 84, 92, 109
addictions, xiv-xv, 32, 72, 76-78, 84, 107-108
anger, 65-67, 74, 108
alone, 1, 29, 31-32, 37, 56, 62, 79, 93, 102
anxiety, 26, 28
anxious, 26, 28
approval seeking, 5, 20

B

binge(d), 21, 95
body, 2, 39, 46, 48, 55-56, 109

C

catharsis, 66, 74, 87, 89
compulsive(ness), 1, 2, 5, 15, 30
confidence, 1, 87, 107

D

Depressed, 26, 95

E

emotional catharsis, 66, 74, 87, 89
emotion(s), 2, 5, 24-25, 28, 36-37
empathy, 72, 88
energy, 15, 27
exciting, 61, 92

F

fear (s), 5, 10-11, 15, 22, 27, 38-40, 44, 46, 51, 61, 66, 73, 87
free, 38, 41, 43, 45, 52, 53
freedom, 44, 72, 102
fun, 14, 49, 56, 60, 92

G

growth, 61, 73, 75, 78, 92, 102
guilt(y), 5, 20, 23, 48-49, 48-49, 51-52, 62, 64, 108

H

healing, 2-4, 39, 54, 76, 88-89, 102-03, 110

---

[2] Page numbers in this Index refer to the printed version of this book. To locate the corresponding page on your e-reader, if necessary do a word search.

home, 4-6, 21-22, 44, 61-62, 79-80, 82, 89, 91-93, 95, 98-99
hopeless, 1, 79

I

inferior, 5, 24
insecurity, 55, 108
isolation, 5, 11

L

lonely, 1, 14, 33, 37, 48, 79, 92,
love, 1, 3-6, 10-11, 14-18, 22, 24, 27-30, 32-33, 39-40, 44-49, 50-51, 54, 57, 59, 61-62, 68-69, 71-77, 84-88, 90-99, 101-104

O

obsessive cycles, 27
overeat(ing), xv, 5, 24, 26, 108
overwhelm(ed), 21, 26

P

pain(ful), 5, 9, 33, 66-67, 84
pillow, 66, 74, 87-89
playing, 59
perfectionism, 5
positive(ly), 2, 11, 30, 69, 101
power, 13, 46, 73. 76
praise, 11, 106-06, 109

R

reassurance, 1, 29, 88
recovery, 4, 94, 107

rejection, 10, 33, 66, 106
relationships, xv, 11, 30-32, 52-53, 107, 109
relaxed, 45, 68, 91
respect, 21, 23-25, 55, 57, 81

S

satisfaction, 6, 73
self-esteem, 5, 23, 27
self-respect, 24, 55, 81, 111
self-worth, 24, 56, 106
starving for love and attention, 11, 14, 17
stress[ed], 25-26, 74, 103, 105, 10
stuffing feelings down inside, 11, 25, 90
substance(s), 12-13, 27, 30, 67, 76-78, 82, 104
success(ful), 10, 23, 33, 50, 57, 63, 77, 102
support, 4, 62, 77-79, 88, 94, 99
survival, 10

U

uncomfortable, 10, 32
unwelcoming, 10

V

vicious cycle, 26
visualizations, 5, 87

W

welcome(d), 95, 99-99
wholesome self-image, 12

www.ingramcontent.com/pod-product-compliance
Lightning Source LLC
Chambersburg PA
CBHW020141130526
44591CB00030B/170